TEACUP IS NOT A
TEACUP

Venerable Master Shen-Kai

Published by

Jen Chen Buddhism Centre
Blk 186, Toa Payoh Central, #01-424, Singapore 310186
bliss@jenchen.org.sg
www.jenchen.org.sg

Cover design and prepress production by Hamlin Associates and Print Run.

For free distribution only
ISBN 978-981-08-2641-3

Distribution Centres

Jen Chen Buddhism Australia Buddhist Bliss Culture Mission
21 Woodthorpe Drive, Willetton, Western Australia 6155
Tel: (61) 8 9354 1245 Fax: (61) 8 9354 4475
Email: contact@buddhistbliss.org.au
www.buddhistbliss.org.au

Jen Chen Buddhist Blissful Culture Centre
30 Lorong 27 Geylang, #05-01/02 Citiraya Centre
Singapore 398582
Tel: (65) 6292 1800 / 6743 1030 Fax: (65) 6844 7719
Email: enquiry@humanbliss.com.sg
www.humanbliss.com.sg

Jen Chen Buddhism Blissful Mission
9691 W. Pacific Ave, Anaheim, CA 92804, U.S.A.
Tel: (714) 775 6078

Jen Chen Buddhist Book Publisher
Towner Road, P.O. Box 0260, Singapore 913229
Tel: (65) 6289 8040 Fax: (65) 6289 2439
Email: juezhong@singnet.com.sg
www.rencheng.com

Jen Chen Buddhism Houston Mission
3159 Bonney Briar Drive,
Missouri City, TX 77459, U.S.A.
Tel: (713) 995 9182
www.jenchen.org

Jen Chen Buddhism Northridge Mission
17500 Nordhoff St, Northridge, CA 91325, U.S.A.
Tel: (818) 775 1231

Jen Chen Buddhism Publisher
39, Sec.2, Dongguang Rd., East Dist.,
Tainan City 701, Taiwan, R.O.C.
Email: jcbook@ms72.hinet.net

About the Author

Venerable Master Shen-Kai was born in 1918, in Guizhou, China. From an early age, he showed extraordinary wisdom and compassion beyond his years. At five, he was able to treat illnesses with herbal remedies. By the time he was seven, his advanced literary ability and insight were evident; standing on Lotus Mountain with his school teacher, gazing over the lands below, he spontaneously composed a piece of poetry which described 'seeing through the illusion of worldly life'. He was enlightened at twelve. In the years that followed, he rapidly advanced through his formal education and graduated from Zhejiang University. By the age of 20, he was head of a county.

Venerable Master Shen-Kai was a tranquil and humble person who radiated a natural warmth that puts people at ease. In his youth, he studied many religions and was so deeply inspired by Buddhism that he became a monk. He devoted his life to rejuvenating Buddhism and creating bliss for humanity. He strongly advocated that as human beings, we must purify our mind, enhance our pure awareness, unfold our wisdom, be upright and moral in our conduct and practise the Bodhisattva Way as the foundation for our quest for supreme enlightenment. Thus, he dedicated his life to promoting Humanity Vehicle Buddhism (Jen Chen Buddhism in Chinese) as expounded by Buddha. Being the first in modern times to have done so, Venerable Master Shen-Kai is honoured as 'The Founding Teacher of World Humanity Vehicle Buddhism' (World Jen Chen Buddhism).

The Venerable Master's wisdom was much sought after and he travelled widely to impart Buddhist teachings. Rather than speaking on a particular topic, he adopted the unique Question and Answer approach with the audience so that he could guide them according to their conditions and levels of understanding. With his profound wisdom, he conveyed the Dharma with such ease and simplicity that people were quickly awakened to its very essence. He penned more than a hundred books on Buddhist practice and established Humanity Vehicle Buddhism Centres in many countries. To this day, his books and magazines on Humanity Vehicle Buddhism continue to be published and received globally. In these, he taught that the culture of Buddhism is in fact a human bliss culture. In gratitude of his dedication in bringing a bliss culture to humanity, Venerable Master Shen-Kai is also revered by many people across nations as the 'Bodhisattva of Bliss'.

The Venerable Master's compassionate vows were magnanimous and far-reaching. He vowed to return to this world lifetime upon lifetime to guide humanity to purify their mind, attain enlightenment and liberation. He hoped that many Bodhisattvas-to-be will be inspired to this effort for a Blissful Pure Land to welcome the birth and supreme enlightenment of Maitreya, the next Buddha.

Venerable Master Shen-Kai
Teacher of Buddhahood Lineage
World Humanity Vehicle Buddhism (Jen Chen Buddhism)

top: Venerable Master Shen-Kai giving a Dharma talk in Singapore.

*bottom: A section of the vast audience at the Dharma talk
held at Westin Hotel, Singapore in 1989.*

Disciples of Venerable Master Shen-Kai in Taiwan, respectfully sending him off as he leaves for Dharma talks in U.S.A.

Officiating a ceremony in U.S.A.

Blessing devotees at an event in Singapore.

Contents

Preface

Teacup is not a Teacup brings together a translation of publications, discussions and public talks which were originally given in Chinese by Venerable Master Shen-Kai, the teacher of Buddhahood Lineage World Jen Chen Buddhism (Humanity Vehicle). In his many years of teaching throughout the world, the Venerable Master became known for his distinctive ability to explain the profound Buddhadharma with such startling clarity and simplicity that audiences would immediately comprehend the Buddha's subtle truths, be able to relate them directly to their own lives and thus benefit themselves and those around them.

The Venerable Master has left a legacy of wisdom in over 100 books that he penned in his native Chinese language. His wisdom continues to be a beacon for many from all walks of life around the globe. With this English translation, we sincerely hope that even more people will have the chance to receive and be awakened by his teachings.

May you attain clarity and insight, and progress along the path of enlightenment.

We wish to acknowledge that some definitions in our endnotes have been adapted from the *Oxford Dictionary of Buddhism* (Keown, 2003), *The Seeker's Glossary of*

Buddhism (Sutra Translation Committee of the United States and Canada, 2003) and *The Shambhala Dictionary of Buddhism and Zen* (Kohn, 1991).

Dharma Translation Council
World Humanity Vehicle Buddhism
(Jen Chen Buddhism)

Buddhahood Lineage
World Humanity Vehicle Buddhism
(Jen Chen Buddhism)

In his lifetime, Śākyamuni Buddha, the founder of Buddhism taught a total of five vehicles of teachings:

1. Humanity Vehicle (pronounced Jen Chen in Chinese)
2. Deva Vehicle
3. Śrāvaka Vehicle
4. Pratyekabuddha Vehicle
5. Bodhisattva Vehicle

'Vehicle' is used in analogy to a mode of conveyance; like a car, ship or airplane which delivers people from one place to another. Humanity Vehicle Buddhism (Jen Chen Buddhism) is the teachings of wisdom that Śākyamuni Buddha preached to humanity.

The word 'Buddha' means 'perfect awareness, fully awakened, fully enlightened'. In the Lotus Sūtra it is stated that *"In the Buddha Lands of the ten directions, there is only one vehicle of teaching. There is no second or third, unless you are speaking of the expedient teachings of the Buddha."* Buddha expounded on five vehicles of teachings to cater for sentient beings' different conditions and levels of understanding. But from the ultimate point of view, there is only one vehicle - the vehicle that leads to supreme enlightenment: Buddhahood Vehicle.

The Buddhahood Lineage was established in hope that we may emulate the Buddha in his cultivation, enhance our self-awareness, attain our innate Buddha-nature and practise Humanity Vehicle Buddhism. By observing Five Precepts[1] and performing Ten Virtuous Deeds[2], we lay foundations ensuring our rebirth in human form lifetime after lifetime, so that we may continually practise the Bodhisattva Way and eventually attain Buddhahood.

Buddhahood Lineage World Humanity Vehicle Buddhism (Jen Chen Buddhism) promotes the original teachings of Śākyamuni Buddha. We pay homage to Śākyamuni Buddha and practise the Way of Bodhisattvas.

The objective of Buddhahood Lineage is to promote Humanity Vehicle Buddhism, to purify the human mind, unfold the innate wisdom of humanity and establish a far-reaching culture of bliss that transforms our impure world into a blissful pure land.

CHAPTER 1

Illusion of name and form

A Dharma talk given by Venerable Master Shen-Kai on 1 Jan 1989 in West Covina, California, USA.

Happy New Year! But that's not to say that if it isn't the New Year, we'll be unhappy. At each moment of the day, if we constantly *'be with Buddha'* (與佛同在), then I believe we will surely be happy everyday.

Before we begin a Dharma talk, why do we usually recite, "Śākyamuni Buddha"? There are two reasons for this. Firstly, Buddhadharma are the teachings bequeathed to us by our teacher, Śākyamuni Buddha. We are here to learn and practise what Buddha taught. Secondly, having travelled quite a distance to attend this talk, some of you are still trying to catch your breath. You've just sat down and your minds are not yet settled. Reciting "Śākyamuni Buddha" will help to settle your mind. In this way, we'll have Buddha in our mind. With Buddha in our mind, I believe that everyone will be able to comprehend the Buddhadharma better.

In teaching Buddhadharma, we find Buddhadharma everywhere. It is inexhaustible. Take this teacup for instance. Even a teacup can lead to an enormous chapter of Buddhist teachings. With Buddhadharma, once you have gained a clearer understanding, you will then be able to see it in its entirety, including all of its different aspects and interconnections.

Buddhadharma is actually very simple. It is the simplest thing to learn, unlike things in this secular world that can be quite troublesome to learn. I mentioned just now that we could expound the Buddhadharma based on a teacup. But how? Well, we could say, "This teacup is not a teacup. It is called a teacup". To explain the teacup, we say that it isn't a teacup and only thus is a teacup. This may sound very contradictory indeed. A teacup and yet not a teacup!? What on earth does this mean? This is a formula of Buddhadharma: *This teacup, not a teacup, is called a teacup.* This teacup-thing isn't a teacup. We named it 'teacup'. We need to realise that 'teacup' is its given name, and this round-shaped glass vessel, its form.

Everything, no matter what it is, has a name and a form. Right now, we are human beings. We have human names and human forms. For example, if your mother had named you Paul at birth, then you would be Paul. If named Kitty, you'd be Kitty. However, in ancient China, children were formally given another name when they began their schooling. So, names are just labels. They are false.

Take another example. People now are called 'human beings'. If at the very beginning, the name had been 'tiger', then perhaps people would now be known as 'tigers' rather than 'human beings'. Therefore, names and forms are false names and false forms.

What about this form called teacup? Today, if this teacup held water, we might be calling it a 'water cup' rather than a 'teacup'. If it held wine, we might be calling it 'wine cup'. If it held soy sauce or vinegar, we might be calling it 'soy sauce dish' or 'vinegar dish'. But because we wish to drink tea, we pour tea into the cup. And so, this vessel is called a 'teacup'. Thus, all names are false.

There are innumerable objects in this world. This is a flower, a lotus flower. This is a table. This is cloth. These are spectacles – but if they are not called spectacles, that would be alright as well. So, all names are false. Everything in this world has a name and a form. Now we are saying that the name 'teacup' is false, it can easily be changed.

But then, what about this form? Clearly, we can see it! We need to understand that everything is made up of earth, water, fire, wind and space. Take a building for example. Its basic material is earth. Our human skin, bone, muscle and hair are all attributed to the earth. Likewise, a teacup has material too. That material is also earth.

Let's say that we have some clay, so we want to make a teacup. But the raw material of clay is earth, which is dry. Without water, it is impossible for us to make a teacup. Thus, having earth, we still require water. Furthermore, we also need to have fire because even if we fashion a teacup from clay, without fire to bake it, the cup cannot be produced. With fire, there needs to be wind. When the fire refuses to burn, a gust of wind gets it going. Finally, we need space. If these seats had not been empty, it would be impossible for us to be seated here. If this table had not been empty, this cup could not be placed on it. Any object anywhere has to occupy a space.

The five elements - earth, water, fire, wind and space, are causes and conditions (*yīn yuán* 因緣). As for the raw materials of these five elements, their beginning is the cause. Earth and water are both causes. The composition of water can further be divided into many components, such as hydrogen, oxygen and minerals. Carbon dioxide is another example. Scientifically speaking, carbon dioxide is made up of many constituents. And the same goes for space. You may perceive the space to be empty. But according to scientific analyses, there are further divisions of components in this space. Earth, water, fire, wind and space are thus known as causes.

What then are conditions? The five elements aggregate as a result of our needs. For instance, because people wanted to drink tea, craftsmen began making cups. Due to our need to use the cups for tea-drinking, they became known as teacups. But if we needed to use the cups for drinking water, then their name would be 'water cups' instead. Since these are unreal names and unreal forms, when the cup is reduced to its constituent parts, the cup does not exist anymore. Thus, it is a false form.

Due to aggregation of causes and conditions, a teacup comes into existence. That was my example. Now, think about this: is there anything in this world that isn't a false name and false form? When you thoroughly understand the principle, you'll find that there's material everywhere to base Dharma talks on, because Buddhadharma is omnipresent. This Law

of Cause and Condition is a Truth. It is one of the Truths
expounded by the Buddha.

Everything in this world is formed by aggregations of earth,
water, fire, wind and space. Likewise for humans, except
humans have an additional quality – *consciousness.*
Therefore, a human being is made up of an aggregation of
earth, water, fire, wind, space and consciousness. *Earth* is
our body. There is muscle, skin, hair, bone, etc; these are all
earth. After we die, our body decomposes and it is still a pile
of earth. *Water* – our tears, blood, sweat and urine are all
water. *Fire* – the fire in our body is our body heat, our
thermal energy. If our body lacked fire, we would not be able
to survive. Human digestion is an endothermic process.
Without heat energy, we cannot digest food. Thus our body
heat is crucial. *Wind* – our body needs wind as well. Wind is
the air that circulates in our body. *Space* – do you know
where the space in human beings is? Human beings need
space. If you don't believe this, try pinching your nose shut.
Without space, air doesn't flow and you will die. Hence, the
whole body is full of spaces. There are skin pores
everywhere and all internal organs have spaces. By the same
token, if this seat hadn't been empty, I couldn't be seated
here now. If this room hadn't been empty, you couldn't be
gathered here today listening to this Dharma talk. So, people
need space. And then humans have something additional -
our *consciousness.* This refers to our ability to discern, to
think. It is also known as soul. When these six kinds of
causes and conditions: earth, water, fire, wind, space and
consciousness aggregate, they form a person. Humans are
produced by the Law of Cause and Condition. What is this
law? Humans have parents. The parents are causes. Because

there is a father, a mother and an additional cause – *consciousness*, when these three kinds of causes and conditions are satisfied, a human being is produced. From the formation of a foetus to a person's death, it has earth, water, fire, wind, space and consciousness.

It is also similar with animals and plants, except that plants are a little bit different. The plant itself is *earth*. Take wood for instance; it grows out of the soil. You would be right to say that the wood is soil, because if you placed a large tree on the ground and left it there for a very long time, you would find nothing left of it later but the pile of soil that it became. It would have decomposed. The human body undergoes a similar process. Look at what happens to a dead body after a few years. It also becomes a pile of soil. Hence, it is also earth. *Water* – without rain and moisture, can trees grow? Trees can't possibly grow. They will wither and die. All trees need water. *Fire* – do you think tree saplings can survive without sunlight? Without sunlight, trees cannot grow to maturity, thus sunlight is also needed. *Wind* is air. When air moves, it becomes wind. Without wind and variations in the air, a tree cannot grow. The same goes for *space*. If there already is a large tree here, it is impossible for you to have another large tree in the same spot, because trees are material objects.

Whilst humans have consciousness or soul, plants have *sense*, which is not the same as consciousness. Plants have an innate sense of light. If a plant grows in a spot with sufficient sunlight, its leaves flourish and take on a vibrant shade of green. Plants without a sense of light have pale leaves and are deficient in certain nutrients. Thus, plants cannot lack earth, water, fire, wind, space and sense. Animals cannot lack earth, water, fire, wind, space and consciousness. Plants and animals differ in this single aspect.

Knowing this principle, can you now think of something that is not formed in this manner? If you can, then this would not be Buddhadharma. But since all animals and plants are produced in this way, this principle cannot be refuted. And since it cannot be refuted, it is a Truth. By Truth, we refer to a real explanation which can neither be repudiated nor debunked. This is what is meant by 'Buddhism speaks the Truth'.

This world is a form produced from aggregations of causes and conditions (因緣相). For example, when a father, a mother and a soul are put together, that constitutes the condition. Due to this condition, a human being is produced. Now, consider this podium. Originally, it did not exist. We couldn't purchase it even if we wanted to. But we needed such a podium, so what was to be done? Fortunately, we had Mr Smith who is a talented man. He repairs cars and can also do a little carpentry. Because Mr Smith knew that we needed a podium, he bought the necessary materials and built this podium himself. Due to these causes and conditions, this podium was produced. If causes and conditions were lacking, I couldn't find any podium and nobody could construct one either, then there would be no podium. Besides, even if Mr Smith had built a podium, if nobody needed it for a lecture, then perhaps his handiwork would only be used at home as a table for a teapot and teacups. It would not be called a podium then. Similarly, everything is produced by specific kinds of causes and conditions. Hence, in this world, all events and objects are merely forms produced by aggregations of causes and conditions. This is the Law of Cause and Condition. It is applicable everywhere. Think about it. Is there anything unrelated to causes and conditions? We might say that nothing is separate from causes and conditions.

Meanwhile, all things and events produced by the aggregation of causes and conditions are also impermanent forms. All things and events produced by the Law of Cause and Condition will eventually return to emptiness. This flower here is blooming very beautifully. We have put it on this podium because it's needed here. If we didn't need it, this flower would not be here. Even this fresh flower itself is an aggregation of causes and conditions; it is a product of earth, water, fire, wind and space. Having been placed here, we presently see a flower. But after a few days, the flower will wilt, decompose and disappear.

If it were an artificial flower, it could serve as a display for a longer period of time. But nevertheless, all material objects ultimately decay. When their time comes, they no longer remain. Thus, all that is formed by the Law of Cause and Condition are unreal and empty. They are all impermanent.

Can you think of anything that exists forever? What will never change and never deteriorate? Please reflect on this.

"What about the air that we breathe?" (A member of the audience asks.)

Is air permanent? There are many places in this world that are in a state of vacuum. There is no air in a vacuum tube. So you see, air changes. If air cannot change, then people would not dare to breathe it either. There is nothing in this world that does not change. Comprehend this principle and you will understand *impermanent form*. Presently, we may observe how beautiful and obedient a child is. But after a few years, that child will be different. And then, look at him again after another fifty years. That child will be an old man or an old lady. Where will that child be then? This is the impermanent form. Everybody is changing from moment to moment, except that we do not realise it.

When a house is built, it is new and vacant. But take another look at it in fifty years' time. The house has changed. Perhaps it is dilapidated. It changes everyday but you do not realise it because the length of a day is too short a time for the change to be apparent. People keep changing everyday too. For example, when you've just shaven off your hair, your head is bald and shiny. But your hair is constantly growing. When it has grown longer, you will shave it off again. Just imagine, since the time when you were an infant, your hair has never stopped growing. Your hair changes everyday throughout your lifetime. This is indicative of the impermanent form. Everything is changing. These impermanent forms are aggregated forms.

What is an aggregated form? The teacup which we mentioned before is an aggregated form produced by the combination of various things. A house is also an aggregation of many materials, such as bricks, tiles, timber, plastics, metal nails, etc. All these are the result of the Law of Cause and Condition. They are all impermanent and aggregated forms. Think about it. What in this world is not an aggregated form? People too, are a combination of earth, water, fire, wind and space. Buildings are an aggregation of things. Even this city of Los Angeles is also an aggregation of a great many causes and conditions. On an even larger scale, this earth is a big aggregated form, and so is the universe. They are not separated from earth, water, fire, wind and space.

When you understand that all things are impermanent, you will not be attached to them. It is because people fail to realise that things are impermanent, that they become so attached to them. Now you know that all these are merely aggregated forms, impermanent forms, and they are forms produced by aggregations of causes and conditions. For instance, a family is also formed by causes and conditions. Because there is a father and a mother, there are then sons and daughters. When there are sons and daughters, there will be grandchildren. Thus a family is formed. But after a few years, due to old age, the elder ones will die and the younger ones will become old. Those not yet born will be born. Family members from the past three or four generations will no longer exist. These are also phenomena of impermanence, causes and conditions, and aggregation. We certainly would not say that the world and all creatures were created by god. If god created everything, then who created god? This doesn't make sense. If you understand these principles, you will be able to embrace Buddhism easily and learn fast. Moreover, if everyone truly comprehends these principles, everyone will be able to speak the Dharma.

Regardless of how you turn things over and examine them, the principles of causes and conditions, aggregation and impermanence will still apply. When you truly understand these principles, you are immediately a Dharma teacher. Why? When you can fully comprehend these principles, you can go on and on for days and nights speaking the Dharma. I have just shared all these with you to elicit your comprehension. From now on, relate these principles to the various situations in your everyday life. Observe everything carefully and you will realise that there is always Buddhadharma there.

Take for example, all these forms that we are seeing now. In the Diamond Sūtra it is taught that all forms that we see are phenomena of arisings and ceasings of many aggregated causes and conditions. That which are continually produced are known as phenomena of arising and ceasing, or sentient beings (眾生). There are inner sentient beings (內眾生) and outer sentient beings (外眾生). Inner sentient beings refer to the thinking in our mind, our opinions and attachments; while outer sentient beings refer to the arising and ceasing of causes and conditions that are outside of our mind, including external beings. When the inner and outer sentient beings (內外眾生) arise continually, this is known as the sentient-being-form (眾生相). There is a statement in the Diamond Sūtra: "*All forms are illusory. Seeing all forms to be non-form is seeing Tathāgata*[3]." Since all forms are unreal and empty, we should empty ourselves of them. When all has emptied away, what is revealed is the Tathāgata.

This Buddha statue that we see before us is a form made of stone. It is a Tathāgata-form, not Tathāgata. The true Tathāgata can only be perceived when we have shattered all forms. Hence, Buddhism is a religion that truly breaks from attachments to form. It is a truly non-superstitious religion. Why do things exist in the world? Buddhism can provide explanations.

In the past, there was a Mahābrahmā Devarāja (king of Mahābrahmā heaven) who liked to tell tall tales. He would often tell the other heavenly beings, "I created human beings. I created the world."

One day, he heard that Buddha had come to the human world and attained Buddhahood; that Buddha knew everything and only spoke the Truth. Thus, Mahābrahmā Devarāja became very curious and decided to go take a look and see what the Buddha was like. From the heavens, he descended to earth. Upon seeing the Buddha, he deliberately paid his respects and asked for guidance on how to practise to achieve liberation.

Because Buddha had the ability to know another's mind, he knew what the Devarāja was up to. So he enquired in return, "Have you ever thought or claimed that you created everything; that you created all sentient beings, made the entire universe and produced heaven and earth?"

The Mahābrahmā Devarāja replied, "Yes, I have thought of that, and have also proclaimed it."

Buddha continued, "Mahābrahmā, who then created you?"

At this point, Mahābrahmā Devarāja was speechless.

Buddha then asked, "You claim to have created all human beings and all life. In that case, is sickness also your creation?"

Afraid to be blamed for sickness, the Devarāja protested, "No, no!"

Because of people's fear of death, Buddha continued to ask, "Since you created life, did you also create death?"

The Devarāja replied, "No, no! I only created life. I didn't create sickness and death."

Buddha proceeded with many more queries which the Devarāja could not answer, so he listened to what the Buddha had to say. As the Buddha spoke, Mahābrahmā Devarāja became both joyous and remorseful. Subsequently, he sought refuge with the Buddha.

Overjoyed, he invited Buddha up to heaven to preach the Dharma. Hence, the first one to have invited Buddha to expound the Dharma in the heavens was Mahābrahmā Devarāja. When Buddha arrived in heaven, there were soon many keen invitations from many other heavens to also have him expound the Dharma there. Once, when Buddha was in Trayastrimśās heaven, Śakra Devarāja (king of Trayastrimśās heaven) took refuge and invited Mahābrahmā Devarāja to his celebration. Soon, all the deva kings in heaven took refuge in Buddha.

Q. In Buddhist jargon, there is a phrase *'conditions arise, their nature is empty* (緣起性空*)'*. What does this mean?

A. Well, *'conditions arise, their nature is empty'* – this is a name-form. Names and forms are false names and false forms after all. If we do not explain this clearly, people tend to seek jargon (i.e. name-forms) from books to explain these terms, consequently making Buddhism sound too profound and too difficult for many to understand. All that I have just shared with you actually explains what is meant by *'conditions arise, their nature is empty'*. Whatever arises from the aggregation of causes and conditions is impermanent. Its nature is empty. Thus, all things and events produced by aggregations of causes and conditions are essentially empty. They are false names and false forms.

— ଐ

CHAPTER 2

There are form and emptiness in the arising and ceasing of causes and conditions

Q. Venerable Master, the sūtra states that, *"Form does not differ from emptiness, emptiness does not differ from form, form is emptiness, emptiness is form"*. **What does this mean? Are there any contradictions?**

A. With regards to 'form' in the phrase, *'form does not differ from emptiness'*, all physical forms that can be seen by our eyes are 'form'. Human beings, animals, plants, buildings, mountains, rivers, mother earth and the myriad of things in the universe are all 'form'. Take for example, the flowers on this podium. They have been formed by the aggregation of causes and conditions. The bouquet is beautiful. There are red flowers, white flowers and green leaves. But after a few days, the flowers will wilt. They will be thrown away into the rubbish dump. In another few days, the flowers in the rubbish dump will decompose. And yet another few days later, they will turn into soil. The flowers will no longer exist. Thus no matter what form, it is eventually empty. That is why *'form does not differ from emptiness'*.

Conversely, *'emptiness does not differ from form'*. Originally, there were no flowers here. The flowers have come into existence from emptiness. Buddhadharma teaches the Law of Cause and Condition. Due to the aggregation of certain causes and conditions, what we now see is a vase of flowers. When these causes and conditions are over, this vase of flowers will cease to exist. Therefore, these four statements from the Heart Sūtra is the Truth. There is no contradiction.

Q. What is the Law of Cause and Condition?

A. The Law of Cause and Condition is very common. You could say that causes and conditions pervade all places, all events and all forms. None of these are separate from Law of Cause and Condition.

To illustrate the Law of Cause and Condition, let us say that the upper and lower storeys of this Buddhist centre are fully packed with the audience of tonight's Dharma talk. This is the Law of Cause and Condition. *Because* Buddhism is a religion for the salvation of humanity, the organisers have invited me here to teach the Buddhadharma. *Because* the public hopes to understand Buddhadharma, *because* as a Buddhist monk I have a responsibility to discuss Buddhadharma with lay Buddhists, and *because* the broad masses all want to seek the Truth of Buddhism and to discuss Buddhadharma; these are the *'causes'*. And today, many have turned up to attend our symposium; these are the *'conditions'*. Countless events in the world are not separated from the Law of Cause and Condition. This is known as *Law of arising and ceasing of causes and conditions*. In every family, why do husbands and wives, parents and children, sisters and brothers have the affinity to be together to make up a family? It is Law of Cause and Condition as well.

To help you understand better, consider this following example. Because many people want to go to Taipei, they all get onto a train. These are *conditions*. However, upon arrival in Taipei, when the train stops at the station, everyone goes their separate ways. These are *'conditions aggregating, conditions dispersing'*. Would you say that the causes and conditions have dispersed? Actually they haven't, this is because new causes and conditions have again formed. Although everybody has alighted from the train, one person is now on his way to a social gathering in the evening, another is on his way to take part in a forum, another is going shopping, another is heading home, another needs to go to a government organisation to sort out some matters, one needs to go to a certain hospital for treatment, etc. And the list goes on and on. This is the arising of other sets of causes and conditions, and the aggregation of other sets of causes and conditions. These causes and conditions are not eternally unchanging. Thus, these are called *'conditions arising, conditions ceasing'*.

'Everything arises due to the aggregation of causes and conditions. Everything ceases due to the dispersal of causes and conditions.' If we need a large building, due to this cause, a large building is built. After many years, because time has passed, we no longer need this large building anymore. This building then changes. It deteriorates and disperses. No matter what it is, nothing can be separate from the Law of Cause and Condition.

Buddhism recognises Causes and Conditions because the Law of Cause and Condition is the Truth.

I hope that each and every one of you will think this over. Of all things, there is nothing that is not the Law of Cause and Condition. Think about it and you will comprehend that absolutely everything in the universe is not separate from the Law of Cause and Condition. This Law of Cause and Condition encompasses positive causes and conditions, as well as negative causes and conditions. When we encounter positive causalities, everything goes well and everything we get is good. However, when we encounter negative causalities, there are a lot of bad things and bad karmic effects.

There is another thing that we also ought to understand: *'Positive causality can be negative causality; negative causality can be positive causality'*. Some of you may be puzzled. How can positive causality be negative causality, and negative causality be positive causality? How does that work? If misfortune befalls someone's family, or if someone's parents have died, this is negative causality. However, because this person now has no one to depend on and no one to help him, he then becomes self-reliant and endeavours to advance himself, work hard and learn. Because of his diligence, he later completes his studies and becomes a useful person in society. Henceforth, his outcome is one of great wealth and prosperity. So, hasn't this negative causality transformed into a positive causality? Conversely, there are people born into wealthy families and very good environments, who spend all their time eating, drinking and being merry instead of working proper jobs. When the day comes that their parents are no longer around, their situation will change and their wealth will disappear. They will then find themselves in difficult straits in their later years. This is how positive causality can be negative causality.

As practitioners of Buddhism, having understood the Law of Cause and Condition, we ought to create new causalities. We should not be sitting around waiting for causalities to arise. Knowing the value of creating good causes and conditions, we must be diligent in our learning and practice, and do things properly. Then naturally, our causalities will be transformed.

We certainly must not have blind beliefs with regards to causes and conditions. Take this situation for an example. Bandits have abducted a girl from your family. If you are resigned to believing that you must submit to these bandits just because it is a causality created in your previous lifetime, then you are deluded about the Law of Cause and Condition, because these bandits should not be abducting anyone's daughter in the first place. If a young man does not engage in proper work but mixes with bad company, he would be wrong to believe these bad friends to be his causality. Thus, we should advocate transforming negative causalities and creating positive causalities. We need to have wisdom in learning and practising Buddhism. With wisdom, we will be able to know whether what we say and do is right or wrong, correct or incorrect. Conversely, if we have no wisdom in learning and practising Buddhism, we may think and conduct ourselves foolishly. Foolish actions eventually lead to distress, suffering and darkness.

While we need to create our causes and conditions, we also need to nurture our positive causes and conditions. This is because throughout countless past lifetimes until this very day, each and every one of us has planted good seeds and bad seeds in our eighth consciousness (also known as ālaya-consciousness or ālaya-vijñāna[4]). The seeds are causes. If we have seeds (causes) that are bad, upon meeting with bad conditions we will become bad people. If we have good seeds, i.e. good causes, and we meet with good people and do good deeds, then these are positive causes and conditions. When we face a negative causality, we must try to transform it into positive causality. And if we meet with a positive causality, we should enhance it further.

Conducting ourselves as humans is similar to farming and cultivating the land. We need to try our best to get rid of the rocks, weeds and other things that are not good. We need to fertilise, water and nurture the crops that we require. If we had blind beliefs about causes and conditions, we would be resigned to weeds being our causality and crops also being our causality. Consequently in future, we would have no harvest at all. Thus, although Buddhism speaks of adapting to conditions, we must nevertheless have wisdom. If we would like to have wisdom, we need to conscientiously cultivate ourselves. Only then will our wisdom unfold.

ॐ

CHAPTER 3

***There is no fixed law
in causes and conditions***

Q. Is the Law of Cause and Condition fixed? Will it change?

A. The Law of Cause and Condition is neither fixed nor not fixed. It is the term '*Cause and Condition*' that is fixed, but their events and circumstances are not. Because the Law of Cause and Condition involves three periods (past, present and future), it is thus also known as the Law of Cause and Effect.

'*Cause*' is the reason, and '*condition*' the aggregation of all factors. Take a tree for example. The seed is the *cause*. After being planted into the ground, it needs to have soil, moisture, sunlight, air, nutrients, etc. It is only with all these *conditions* that the seed sprouts, grows, flowers and bears fruit. This is the Law of Cause and Condition. Is the Law of Cause and Condition always fixed in this manner? All matters that involve the Law of Cause and Condition work this way.

There is also '*Differential Cause and Condition*'. For example, if we planned to grow a certain crop this year but coincidentally, there is lack of rain; this would be the case of Differential Cause and Condition. Here's another example. Some people believe that if they had a son, they would send him to school with the hope that he would turn out to be highly educated and eventually hold a high-ranking ministerial position. However, if they indeed had a son, but it turned out that he was not good at his studies, then this would also be Differential Cause and Condition. There is no guarantee that he would certainly excel in his studies and become a minister. Each has his own causes and conditions.

And then there is also the *'Condition which arises from related condition'*. For example, because there is a mother, she can therefore give birth to a son. And because her son has an income, he can in turn take care of his mother's daily expenses.

There is much to the Law of Cause and Condition. We could say that the conditions are fixed. We could also say that they are not. There is a saying in Buddhism, *"The Law of Cause and Condition is not fixed. That which is fixed is not Law of Cause and Condition."* Since that which is fixed is not Law of Cause and Condition, and everything is part of the Law of Cause and Condition, thus under certain causes and conditions, certain teachings will be taught. The Law of Cause and Condition is impermanent, arising and ceasing because conditions change. Hence, if Buddhadharma is unchanging, that is not Buddhadharma, because Buddhadharma is aimed at treating the various arisings of the mind. If there is no mind, there is no need for Buddhadharma.

બ

CHAPTER 4

Impermanence

Since ancient times, people all over the world, regardless of race, nationality and gender, as well as celestial beings in heaven, have longed for eternity. We wish that our lives will be long and our wealth and belongings will remain with us forever, untouched by deterioration. *'Impermanence'* is the most terrifying and detestable thing to us. This was exemplified by what happened in Chinese history, during the Qin dynasty (221 B.C. – 210 B.C.). There was the foolish and unethical Emperor Qin Shi Huang who burned books, harmed educated people and built the Great Wall of China. With fantasies of his own immortality, he sent an envoy of 3,000 virgin boys and girls, led by his court sorcerer, Xu-Fu, all the way to Japan to find an elixir of immortality to satisfy his desire for an eternal life so that he could be emperor forever.

In our world, how could things be forever unchanging? Moment to moment, time passes by; everything changes continuously and ceaselessly. All things and events arise by aggregations of causes and conditions, and cease again by dispersals of causes and conditions. All living beings go through *'birth, aging, sickness and death'*. Every event and thing in our world goes through *'arising, abiding, changing and extinction'*. A new and beautiful object or a luxurious building is constantly in the midst of change. After a few years or a few decades, you will see that it has aged and deteriorated. Even the world in which we live also goes through *'formation, existence, destruction and void'*. It never ceases to change. Finally, it will be destroyed. The svelte young lady whom you remember from thirty years ago has already aged and become jaded like a yellowed pearl. And the handsome young man from back then is now greying at the temples. At 70-80 years of age, who is not hard-of-hearing and poor-sighted? Who does not have weak teeth, white-hair, a hunched back and the laboured movements of an aged person? Old and ailing like a candle guttering in the wind, one could perish any moment. Having lived a century, people finally will die. On the road of the netherworld, there are many in their prime. Yesterday there were trifle arguments and calculative concerns. Today, with the arrival of *'impermanence'*, we leave empty-handed. What we take with us are not the darling wives, beautiful concubines, beloved children, good grandchildren, wealth, the luxurious houses, status or power. Rather, it is all the virtuous and evil karma that we have committed in our life. If we have been virtuous, we rise to heaven and enjoy happiness. If we have been evil, we descend to hell and suffer.

Even in heaven, when the blessings of the heavenly beings are exhausted, nearing their death, five signs of celestial decline begin to appear: 1) their celestial clothes become very soiled, 2) the garland of flowers on their heads begin to wither, 3) perspiration exudes continuously from their armpits, 4) their bodies lose the majestic radiance and become unbearably smelly, and 5) they can no longer appreciate their treasured seats like before. Those who have evil karma will then descend into hells of copper walls and iron pillars, immense forests of swords and blade-like mountains, flaming pots of burning oil and beds of nails, bitter cold and fiery heat. There is continuous unspeakable suffering. A human rebirth is very difficult to come by. Since we are already human beings in this lifetime, why not make the most of our precious human life to perform more virtuous deeds and refrain from committing evil actions, so as to sow our blessings?

As practitioners, not only do we seek humanly or heavenly blessings (which are still subject to transmigration, arising and ceasing, and thus are not the ultimate), but we should also advance a step further to pursue the Truth taught by Buddha and unfold the wisdom innate and complete in us. Cultivating both blessings and wisdom, let us board the 'ship of compassion' quickly and sail across the sea of suffering to attain utmost joy. Only the pure lands of the Buddhas everywhere are truly refreshing, peaceful, stable, auspicious, ultimate, perfect and complete. Only upon reaching the other shore will we forever part with the suffering of cyclic transmigration in the six realms[5], and be free from the shackles of impermanence. Only in the brightness of Tathāgata[3] can we have boundless life, never-ending peace and happiness, inexhaustible blessings, everlasting ease and eternal bliss.

ॐ

CHAPTER 5

Eight kinds of suffering

For people who are older or have possessed wisdom from an early age, based on what they have personally experienced and realised, or what they have observed by their wisdom, none of them would say that life is completely happy. The happiness of our human world is after all, transient, illusory, empty and without true nature. As humans, we must know that once we have a physical body, it will be the source of our distress and suffering. Nobody could fortuitously avoid suffering. There are innumerable sentient beings; so too are their vexations and anguish immeasurable. The suffering that is common knowledge and common sights to all of us may be divided into the following categories: birth, aging, sickness, death, unfulfilled desires, separation from loved ones, being with those we resent and dislike, and the flames of the five Skandhas[6]. Together, these are the eight kinds of suffering.

A person's life begins when the soul consciousness enters the embryo. Six sense organs gradually develop. Being in the womb is similar to being inside an earthen jar; you are in a darkness where no daylight gets in, and you cannot stretch yourself out. For the pregnant mother, her belly swells up and she experiences increasing difficulties in mobility, poor appetite and nausea, all of which she must force herself to endure. Giving birth to the baby, the mother hovers between life and death; her pain so excruciating it is as if the ground were cleaving and mountainous landslides were taking place. It is like being in a slaughterhouse. When the baby emerges and its tender flesh comes into contact with moving air, it feels as if its body is being scrapped with knives. Being bathed and clothed feels more like being pricked. So, a newborn baby screams and cries. This is the '*suffering of birth*'.

When a person gets old, physical strength deteriorates, the limbs become feeble, black hair turns white, sight is not sharp, hearing gets unclear, teeth fall out, the mind is hazy, movements are infirm with age, and nothing goes the way you want it to. Always distressed and in mental anguish, you sigh in despair. This is the '*suffering of aging*'.

A person's body is made of an aggregation of the four elements: earth, water, fire and wind. Muscles and tendons, bones, skin, flesh, internal organs, arteries and veins, fingernails and hair – all the solids constitute the earth element. Blood, urine, sweat and tears – the liquids constitute the water element. Body-heat and thermal energy constitute the fire element. Breathing and the circulation of air through our body constitute the wind element. When the four elements are in balance, body and mind are healthy. When the four elements are out of balance, or when there are injuries, then worries and distress arise. This is the '*suffering of sickness*'.

Everyone eventually dies; it is only a matter of time. Even if you lived to a hundred, death would still claim you in the end. For humanity, our wishful thinking, craving and clinging, anger, terror, hatred, debts, immoral conduct and all kinds of attachments intensify our fear of dying. So, upon death when we suffer the effects of our negative karma, we suffer it multifold. This is the '*suffering of death*'.

Because people's greed and craving have become habitual, we have never-ending wants and desires. When our presumptuous expectations are unmet, vexations and suffering arise in our minds and hearts. For example, scheming in vain for the greed for material wealth, craving for women, undeserved reputations, etc, crimes are foolishly committed and legal punishment received. Thus, you suffer physical and mental agony. This is the '*suffering of unfulfilled desires*'.

Because people are bound by entanglements of love and strong emotional attachments to family, those of us who are deeply attached to our parents, spouses, siblings and children suffer grief, vexation, distress and depression when we have to part with loved ones, or when someone dies. This is the '*suffering of separation from loved ones*'.

People have a tendency to fight over what is right and wrong. Thus, disputes and litigations are commonplace. When feuding families or enemies meet, they silently stare one another down, with hatred and fury burning in their hearts. Their wrath is also physically evident in their outward appearances. Their torment is beyond words. What arises is the '*suffering of being with those we resent and dislike*'.

Due to contact made with our eyes, ears, nose, tongue, body and mind (our six sense organs); form, feeling, thinking, mental activity and consciousness (five Skandhas) arise in our minds and hearts. There is a tangle of distress and suffering which compounds and grows increasingly severe. This is known as the '*suffering of the flames of the five Skandhas*'.

In any case, from birth to death, no one can avoid all this suffering. Furthermore, due to greed, anger, ignorance, arrogance, suspicion, etc, that exists between people, a boundless sea of suffering has been created. Buddha has compassion and empathy for sentient beings. For the sake of delivering us from suffering, he made clear to us the ultimate and supreme way to enlightenment. Only when we are aware of suffering, detest it, are determined to free ourselves from it and embark on the ship of salvation heading across to the shore of enlightenment, will we be able to leave this Sahā[7] world's sea of suffering and be soothed, settled, happy, at peace, dignified and at ease in the inner pure land of utmost bliss, where suffering is absent forever more.

CHAPTER 6

Ceasing the links of dependent origination

When Śākyamuni Buddha was in Hualin hall of Hualin Cave telling a group of Bhiksus[8] stories of previous lives of Buddhas, he spoke of a past kalpa[9] when Vipaśyin Buddha had been a prince. After being ordained by a Śramana[10], he travelled with a group of monks from village to village, country to country. No matter where he went, people always respected him and made reverent offerings to him. It then occurred to Vipaśyin Bodhisattva, "It is very noisy amidst masses of people." Thereafter, he found a quiet secluded place and practised diligently, contemplating day and night.

One day, with his wisdom he observed how sentient beings of the world are constantly in darkness. "Birth, aging, sickness and death; we are forced to suffer much anguish. Life is fragile. Having come from elsewhere, we were reborn here; having died here, we will be reborn elsewhere. Because of suffering stemming from our five Skandhas[6], there is transmigration in the six realms[5]; birth and death stream continuously one after the other. There is no reprieve. This suffering is endless; truly piteous, truly lamentable. I wonder when sentient beings will become aware of the five Skandhas creating their suffering, and practise diligently to eventually cease the suffering of their cyclic existence in the stream of never-ending birth and death."

And then he thought, "What is the cause of sentient beings'

birth and death? Ah, I understand! It is due to *'birth' (jati)* that there is *'aging and death' (jara-marana)*. Tracing to the source, birth is the *'cause'*, aging and death the *'conditions'*. However, why does *'birth'* arise? It is due to *'becoming' (bhava)* that it arises. Thus, *'becoming'* is the condition for *'birth'*. And where does *'becoming'* arise from? It arises from *'grasping' (upadana)*. Thus, *'grasping'* is the condition for *'becoming'*. And why does *'grasping'* arise? Because *'grasping'* arises from *'craving' (trsna)*, *'craving'* is therefore the condition for *'grasping'*. And why does *'craving'* arise? *'Craving'* arises because of *'feeling' (vedana)*, thus *'feeling'* is the condition for *'craving'*. And how does *'feeling'* arise? *'Feeling'* arises from *'contact' (sparsa)*, thus *'contact'* is the condition for *'feeling'*. And where does *'contact'* arise from? *'Contact'* arises from the eyes, ears, nose, tongue, body and mind, i.e. entry through our six senses. Thus, these *'six sense entries' (sad-ayatana)* are the conditions for *'contact'*. And how do the *'six sense entries'* arise? *'Six sense entries'* arise because of sight, sound, smell, taste, touch and thought, i.e. all *'name and form' (nama-rupa)*. Thus, all *'name and form'* are the conditions for *'six sense entries'*. However, why do all *'name and form'* arise? Because *'name and form'* arise from *'consciousness' (vijñāna)*, thus *'consciousness'* is the condition for all *'name and form'*. And why does *'consciousness'* arise? *'Consciousness'* arises because of *'mental activity' (samskara)*, thus *'mental activity'* is the condition for *'consciousness'*. And why does *'mental activity'* arise? Because of *'ignorance' (avidya)*, it arises. Thus, *'ignorance'* is the condition for *'mental activity'*. This *'ignorance'* is the absence of clarity and brightness.

"So it is as such. Because there is *ignorance*, so there is *mental activity*. Because of *mental activity*, there is *consciousness* (discrimination). Because of *consciousness*, there are *name and form*. Because of *name and form*, there are *six sense entries*. Because of *six sense entries*, there is *contact*. Because of *contact*, there will be *feeling*. Because of *feeling*, there is then *craving*. Because of *craving*, there is the want to *grasp*. Because of *grasping*, there is *becoming*. Because of *becoming*, there is *birth*. Because of *birth*, there are suffering and anguish of aging, sickness and death, as well as the mental state of worry, sadness and distress. Suffering from five Skandhas as such, has stemmed from the arising of a thought, which then accumulated to multitudes of suffering."

And then he thought, "Such a development for sentient beings is truly too distressing. What method can we use so that there will be no more worry, sadness and sorrow, and the suffering of aging, sickness and death?" With his wisdom, he observed and was illuminated with awakening. "Ah! Without *'birth'*, there is no anguish of aging, sickness and death. If *'birth'* ceases, the suffering from aging and death also naturally ceases. Without *'becoming'*, there is no *'birth'*. Thus, if *'becoming'* ceases, it follows that *'birth'* ceases. Without *'grasping'*, there is no *'becoming'*. Thus ceasing *'grasping'* also ceases *'becoming'*. Without *'craving'*, there is no *'grasping'*. Ceasing *'craving'* therefore ceases *'grasping'*. Without *'feeling'*, there is also no *'craving'*. Ceasing *'feeling'* therefore ceases *'craving'*. And if we do not come into *'contact'*, there is naturally no *'feeling'*. If we do not use our eyes, ears, nose, tongue, body and mind, i.e. entry through these six senses, these *'six sense entries'* cease, and thus *'contact'* also ceases. If we do not take in sight, sound, smell, taste, touch and thought, there are no *'names and forms'*; therefore there are no *'six sense entries'*. Because *'names and forms'* cease, so too do the *'six sense entries'* cease. If the discriminating *'consciousness'* ceases, there will be no myriad of terminology and forms. Thus, when *'consciousness'* ceases, *'name and form'* also cease. If there is no *'mental activity'*, then there is no discriminating *'consciousness'*. Ceasing *'mental activity'* therefore ceases *'consciousness'*. If each and every sentient being has no *'ignorance',* not a thought arises and there is constant illumination of pure awareness, then there isn't any behaviour or action that brings about suffering.

"In conclusion, *ignorance* ceases, thus *mental activity* ceases. *Mental activity* ceases, thus *consciousness* ceases. *Consciousness* ceases, thus *name and form* cease. *Name and form* cease, thus *six sense entries* cease. *Six sense entries* cease, thus *contact* ceases. *Contact* ceases, thus *feeling* ceases. *Feeling* ceases, thus *craving* ceases. *Craving* ceases, thus *grasping* ceases. *Grasping* ceases, thus *becoming* ceases. *Becoming* ceases, thus *birth* ceases. *Birth* ceases, thus so do aging, death, worry, sorrow, anguish, etc. All ceases."

Vipaśyin Bodhisattva contemplated as such. The five Skandhas extinguished completely. Then arose *'knowledge'*, arose *'insight'*, arose *'pure awareness',* arose *'realisation'*, arose *'complete clarity'*, arose *'wisdom'* and arose *'attainment of enlightenment '*. Thus, observing the twelve links of Dependent Origination forwards and backwards, knowing as such, seeing as such, instantly there was no arising and no ceasing. Brightness of pure awareness illuminated, and on his seat Vipaśyin Bodhisattva attained supreme Buddhahood.

CHAPTER 7

Buddhism is a religion that truly transcends forms and idols

Q. The Diamond Sūtra states, *"If one sees me by forms or seeks me in sounds, one is practising the wrong path and cannot perceive the Tathāgata[3]"*. **What does this mean?**

A. The Diamond Sūtra states, *"If one sees me by forms or seeks me in sounds, one is practising the wrong path and cannot perceive the Tathāgata"*. And it further states that, *"All forms are illusory. Seeing all form to be non-form is seeing Tathāgata"*. The profound meaning of these verses can only be truly realised at a more advanced stage of Buddhist practice. If we were to speak in such a way to a beginner, he would find it too profound to comprehend. A person who has only begun to learn Buddhism really does not know how the Buddha looks like. However, he knows how humans look like, and thus he assumes that only a figure that looks human-like is Buddha. Is his notion correct? We could say that it is, and it isn't.

Consider this example of kindergarten children. When the teacher speaks of grandparents, some children may not know what grandparents look like. So the teacher has to hold up a drawing to point out to them, "This old man is like your grandpa. This old lady is like your grandma." Thereafter, when the children see elderly men and women who resemble the drawings, they know that those are somebody else's grandparents. They also know that their own grandparents look that way too.

If they were university students, their professor would talk of grandparents in terms of blood relations and ancestry. They would understand such an explanation. However, if their professor were to use the kindergarten teacher's method of showing them a drawing and explaining, "This is an old man, just like grandpa. This is an old lady, just like grandma", the students would find it very strange indeed. They would think, "Come on, we're university students now and the professor's lecturing this way?" Wouldn't that be a joke? Thus, that would be very unsuitable indeed.

Hence, the same applies to the learning of Buddhism. To a person who is new to Buddhism, we may initially say, "There is a statue of Buddha in the temple. Go pay your respects to Buddha." And so this person goes to pay her respects to Buddha. When she looks upon the Buddha's statue and observes that he resembles a human being, she is not afraid. Moreover, joy and reverence arise in her heart when she sees the majesty, dignity and compassionate countenance of the images of Buddhas and Bodhisattvas. She is then inspired to learn Buddhism.

After learning Buddhism for a long time, some people may say such things as, "I had a dream. I saw the image of a certain Buddha again. I saw the arrival of a Bodhisattva!" Initially, when you do not know the level of their understanding of Buddhism, you may praise them, "Oh! You must have such good affinity with the Buddha and Bodhisattva that you have been able to see their images!" But if you were to continue praising them like that all the time, it would not be right. If they have such dreams thrice or more, you should tell them, "Mara[11] has come, you've seen Mara!" At this juncture, that is what you should say. In the Zen kōan[12], the Zen master said that if Buddha comes, cut Buddha off. If Mara comes, cut Mara off. You must no longer praise them, because they are already harbouring attachments to form.

Similarly, if they have reached very advanced levels in their Buddhist practice, we should no longer use the kindergarten method. Instead, we should use the Diamond Sūtra method, i.e. *'If one sees me by forms or seeks me in sounds, one is practising the wrong path and cannot perceive the Tathāgata'*. Alternatively, *'All forms are illusory. Seeing all forms to be non-form is seeing Tathāgata'*. Having reached this stage, one realises that Buddhism is a religion that truly transcends delusions and forms.

Some people regard the image of Buddha as an idol, and readily criticise that Buddhism is about idol-worshipping. But are there any religions that do not make use of idols and images? The crucifix is also an idol, the image of Jesus Christ is also an idol, and so is the image of Mother Mary. We cannot say that images are used only in Buddhism. Actually, in Buddhism, there is no idol-worshipping because we understand that *'All forms are illusory. Seeing all form to be non-form is seeing Tathāgata.'*, as was expounded in the Diamond Sūtra. The Tathāgata-essence, Buddha nature completely permeates spacious Dharmadhātu. Dharma nature pervades spacious emptiness.

CHAPTER 8

Pure mind - pure land,
our innate nature Amitabha

'Amitabha' means boundless brightness, boundless life, boundless merit[13]; in fact, a boundlessness of everything good. Most of us only know Amitabha Buddha to be the Dharma Teacher of the Western Pure Land of Utmost Bliss. However, we may not realise that all of us also have in us our own Pure Land and Amitabha. Since in our mind there is Amitabha Buddha, how should we then cultivate ourselves in order to uncover our *innate nature Amitabha*?

Take for example when someone casts abusive language at me, I recite "Amitabha Buddha". This indicates that not only do I not receive his abuse, but in reciting "Amitabha Buddha", boundless brightness is revealed, eliminating the darkness arising from his abusive language.

Similarly, when I'm given a present, I say "Amitabha Buddha". This expresses my gratitude. At this time, our minds are filled with boundless brightness and the giver also receives boundless blessings. Therefore, we resonate with Amitabha Buddha.

When I observe that a person has a dignified appearance, good-looking countenance, and is kind and gracious, I say "Amitabha Buddha". This expresses my commendation of the person for his virtuous qualities as Amitabha Buddha himself is very majestic, dignified, handsome, kind and gracious. In saying "Amitabha Buddha", I am praising the person for his majesty and dignity akin to Amitabha Buddha.

When I see a student studying, I say "Amitabha Buddha". Of course, we could also say, "He is very conscientious and intelligent!" However, sometimes an intelligent person may be adversely obstructed by his intelligence. An intelligent person who does well at school may not necessarily go on to do good things when he grows up. If we use "Amitabha Buddha" to express our praise for such a person, brightness arises in his mind. With brightness of mind, not only will he be able to study well and do great things, but in future when he grows up, he will go on to practise as a Bodhisattva and eventually attain Buddhahood. Hence, praising one by saying "Amitabha Buddha" is indeed excellent.

What if we come across a slaughter house where pigs, cattle or other animals are killed? Any killing constitutes committing a transgression which will cause one to descend into hell. When you see this and say, "They slaughter these animals, so they will go to hell!", do you think these are appropriate words to say for that moment? Whether the other party goes to hell or not, we do not know. However, by saying, "go to hell", we ourselves are already resonating with hell. Because there is darkness and suffering in hell, by making such a statement, we resonate with the darkness and suffering of hell. Conversely, if we say "Amitabha Buddha", there is instantly brightness in our minds and the image of the slaughter house does not take root in our mind.

If we see two people quarrelling or fighting with each other, we must not join in. If we take part in such activities, in

58

future we will end up in the asura realm. Going to the asura realm is not good. All we need to do is to think of Amitabha Buddha and recite "Amitabha Buddha", then in the future we will not resonate with beings of the asura realm.

At a market place, we may notice people short-changing others or cheating on the scales. These are all actions of deceit. Just saying "Amitabha Buddha" would suffice. Because short-changing others and cheating on the scales are actions of greed, these are in resonance with the realm of ghosts. In future such people will fall into the realm of ghosts. By reciting "Amitabha Buddha", not only do we not resonate with ghosts, but furthermore, we resonate with Amitabha Buddha and have boundless brightness.

All over the world, curiosity is a common human trait. When we discover that someone has a secret, we might steal an extra glance to satisfy our curiosity. Although this in itself is not such a serious matter, it would be terrible if we witnessed the other party getting up to something bad! If they found out, our life could be over. But conversely, if we just mentally recite, "Amitabha Buddha" and quickly take our leave, we would be in resonance with all virtue and brightness, rather than with darkness.

If we see that someone has fallen into water, of course we should save him if we have the ability to do so. However, if we lack the ability, and someone else goes to his rescue, we can help by saying, "Amitabha Buddha". This will bring the brightness and blessings of Amitabha Buddha to the victim. Furthermore, in our own mind, we would be in resonance with Amitabha Buddha.

If someone tells you how bad Mrs Jones or Mrs Smith is, whether or not they are bad, that is their own business. In the Platform Sūtra of the 6th Patriarch Hui Neng, it is stated that, *"Although I see another's fault, with his erring I do not myself err. Else, my own erring is a fault."* That is to say, if someone has committed a wrong-doing, that is their own affair. If I were to join in and participate in the wrong-doing, then I would have committed an offence. When you hear this person speaking ill of others, it would suffice just to say, "Amitabha Buddha". Otherwise, if upon hearing these complaints, you speak ill of the others too, then this person may very well go over to the other side and speak badly of you! By simply saying, "Amitabha Buddha", you resonate with brightness and nobody has reason to create trouble or to speak ill of you.

Hence, "Amitabha Buddha" really is a very useful phrase. Regardless of whether we encounter good, bad or neutral situations, we say "Amitabha Buddha". Then, our mind is at ease and in brightness. Henceforth, we resonate with brightness.

We should cultivate this good habit of reciting "Amitabha Buddha", but it isn't very easy to do! Because, if you only recite "Amitabha Buddha" with your lips and not with your mind, that will not do. You should always maintain brightness of mind and constantly be in resonance with Amitabha Buddha. In this way, while you say "Amitabha Buddha", the karma of your body, speech and mind are all in resonance with Amitabha Buddha.

Actually, attaining brightness of mind is simple. This is how you need to practise: *'Mind of the past cannot be grasped; mind of the present cannot be grasped; mind of the future cannot be grasped'*. The mind of the past has already passed, you cannot catch it back. The mind of the future has yet to arrive, so you cannot grab hold of it, much as you may want to. The mind of the present does not stay. No matter what is on your mind now, as soon as the next thought arises, it would already have gone. Thus, you have no way of holding on either. So, all the same, we will need to cultivate non-ego, to shatter our *'I'* ego. With the notion of 'I', there will be a 'my'. Thus, you think, "*My* wife, *my* husband, *my* house, *my* assets, *my* children, etc". Everything is *'mine'*. But where is this *'I'*? You cannot even be sure. Take a moment now, close your eyes and search for *'I'*. *(two minutes' silence follows…)*

Did you find *'I'*? Because this *'I'* is truly hard to find, no matter where you search throughout your whole body, you will fail to discover where it is. If you say, "I see you, Venerable", then is it your *'I'* that is seeing? You may reply that, "The *'I'* who sees are my eyes." But then again, that would be *my* eyes that see, rather than the *'I'* that sees. If you say, "I hear you teaching the Dharma, Venerable", what hears are *my* ears. It is not the *'I'* that hears. Eyes are not the *'I'*, and neither are ears. But even if eyes and ears were *'I'*, how about the nose? Who is that? If you think that your nose is *'I'*, then who is the mouth? Nevertheless, you have to say "*my* mouth"! If you say that the mouth is *'I'* and the tongue is *'I'*, then who are the arms and legs? They are all *'my* arms and *my* legs'. Even the hairs on the head are regarded as 'the hair on *my* head'. In that case, you may perhaps consider your head to be the *'I'*. But if you say that the head is *'I'*, then again, who is the body? No matter how we discuss these, they are all not *'I'*. Since they are not *'I'*, it would appear that there is no reason to be attached to an *'I'* at all. Therefore, as practitioners, we must constantly seek out *'non-I'* form. Everywhere is non-ego. With the discovery of *'non-I'* form, comes the realisation of illusory forms and illusory *'I'* everywhere.

And then, there is the *'non-person'* form. By a *'person'* form, we are referring to the other person, relative to ourselves. Since we cannot even find an *'I'* form, how could we possibly find a *'person'* form? Thus, the *'person'* form is empty. If the *'I'* form is empty, then of course the *'person'* form of the other party is also empty. Furthermore, if *'I'* form and *'person'* form are all empty, then how could there be *'sentient being'* form? Therefore, we say that the form of sentient beings is also empty. What is *'sentient being'* form? *'Sentient being'* form encompasses both inner beings and outer beings. Inner beings refer to the thinking in our mind, our opinions and attachments; while outer beings refer to the arising and ceasing of causes and conditions that are external to our mind, including all people. Since the *'sentient being'* form is empty, so too is *'time'* form. That too is empty. A practitioner needs to practise until he has attained *'no Three Minds and no Four Forms'*. The mind of the past cannot be grasped, the mind of the present cannot be grasped, the mind of the future cannot be grasped; no *'I'* form, no *'person'* form, no *'sentient being'* form, no *'time'* form – that is what is meant by *'no Three Minds and no Four Forms'*. When you have freed yourself of all forms and realised the empty nature of everything, then in this state of emptiness there is boundless brightness. When you attain this boundless brightness, Amitabha Buddha resides in your mind.

Everyone has an illusory *'I'*. Since this body is false, merely an aggregated form, we should make better use of it to cultivate ourselves, attain merits and perform meritorious deeds. In performing meritorious deeds, we do not just do them today and stop tomorrow. In the past, we should have done them. We should do them in the present too, and also in the future. Similarly, morals and ethics are what we ought to have in the past, present as well as future. Since there is boundless brightness and boundless merit, so past... present... future... past... present... future..., this is *'boundless time'*.

Thus, we have attained our own *'innate nature Amitabha'*. At this juncture, although we have not yet reached the Western Pure Land of Utmost Bliss and we are still living at home, our home has already become a part of the Western Pure Land of Utmost Bliss.

What is *'Pure Land'*? The lands of the Buddhas in the ten directions are known as Pure Lands. Where do Pure Lands come from? First, we start by purifying the mind. There is only a Pure Land when the mind is pure. Our mind is similar to the mother earth. In Chinese, when we say that a person is kind-hearted, we might say that the field of his mind is very good, the grounds of his mind are bright. The mind is compared to fields and lands because out of fields and lands, a multitude of plants can grow. Likewise, from within our minds spring all kinds of intentions, all kinds of solutions. Heavens and hells are created by the mind. If in your mind you think only virtuous thoughts, then what you do will also be virtuous. Consequently, you rise to the heavens. If you think evil thoughts, you will come up with evil intentions, do evil things and thus descend into hell. Therefore, heavens and hells are all creations of the mind. Now, if neither good nor bad abides within the mind, it is pure. *'Pure mind, pure land.'* When everybody's mind has become pure, the land upon which we live will also be pure.

Those who wish to be reborn in the Western Pure Land of Utmost Bliss should not think that they can be reborn there with whatever karma they have. Actually, it all depends on what kind of karma it is. With virtuous karma, rebirth will be in a virtuous realm. With evil karma, rebirth will be in an evil realm. It is only with pure karma that one will be reborn in the Western Pure Land of Utmost Bliss. Because, everything that we do is karma; there is body karma, speech karma and mind karma (the three karmas). Only when our body, speech and mind are all pure, will we be able to be reborn in the Western Pure Land of Utmost Bliss. While reciting "Amitabha Buddha", we can attain purity of three karmas. When one's mind becomes pure, one's surroundings will respond positively. When every person purifies his mind, the family becomes pure. When families are pure, society becomes pure. When societies are pure, the country becomes pure. And when countries are pure, we have a pure world. Thus, pure land on earth will be accomplished.

For those of us who practise by reciting the Buddha's name, it is important that we also cultivate all kinds of blessings. As is said in Amitabha Sūtra, *"to be born in this Pure Land, one must not be lacking in virtuous roots, blessings, causes and conditions"*. When we have accomplished the six perfections (Six Pāramitās), i.e. morality, forbearance, generosity, diligence, dhyāna-samādhi[14] (禪 定) and wisdom, to be reborn in the Western Pure Land will be a simple matter. If your mind has become as pure as Amitabha Buddha's, you need not wait for Amitabha Buddha to bring you to the Pure Land. At that point, you already are a Great Bodhisattva. Not only can Great Bodhisattvas go to the Western Pure Land, they can also go to any pure land in the ten directions.

If you practise in this way, when you reach the Western Pure Land, you will not be born of a lower calibre in a lower lotus grade. On the contrary, you may be born of a higher calibre in a higher lotus grade, or even surpass lotus grades altogether to become a teacher there.

CHAPTER 9

Purity of three karmas

'*Karma*' means action. For any action that we commit, if it is of a virtuous nature, it will bring about the result of happiness. If it is of a wicked or unwholesome nature, it will bring about the effect of suffering. These kinds of virtuous and evil natures are known as '*karmic causes*' for happiness and suffering. Having these karmic causes, when we encounter various opportunities to act upon them, we have what is known as '*karmic condition*'. The resulting happiness and suffering that these karmic conditions produce are '*karmic fruit*' of virtue and evil.

We human beings, regardless of gender and age, commit karma in our daily lives which fall into three categories: body, speech and mind. These are known as the '*three karmas*'. '*Body karma*' is the virtuous or evil actions produced by movements of our body and limbs. '*Speech karma*' is performed via the beautiful or ugly sounds produced by the tongue within our mouth. From our mind, the thoughts that are produced, which are good, bad, virtuous, evil, etc, are known as '*mind karma*'. Thus, mind karma is also the driving force of body karma and speech karma.

The word '*mind*' also possesses the meaning of '*thinking*', which is why the two words, '*thinking mind*' are often used together. There are three kinds of thinking, first of which is '*deliberation*'. Before body or speech karma occur, deliberation first takes place, "Can this be done or not? Should this be said or not?" This careful consideration is known as deliberation. The second kind of thinking is '*decision-making*', which refers to deciding to do something or not to do something, to say something or not to say something. The third kind of thinking is '*pre-action rationalising*'. Before acting, we consider, "Performing virtues is right and performing vices is wrong." And before speaking, we consider, "It is right to say something good and wrong to say something bad." Such considerations are known as '*pre-action rationalising*'. As for our speech and actions, the old Chinese adage goes, "You must think thrice before you act!" The aforementioned 'think thrice' is in effect, the three kinds of thinking which we have just discussed.

We should think thrice before we speak and act. Having thought thrice, we should select the virtuous and beneficial to act upon, and abandon the harmful and unwholesome. Because virtuous speech and actions will surely bring about happy karmic effects, they are called '*karma of blessings*'. Because wicked and unwholesome speech and actions will surely bring about karmic effects of suffering, they are called '*karma of misfortune*'. Practitioners, who practise as such, because of their profound dhyāna-samādhi[14] (禪定), will cause their karma to become virtuous and beneficial. Thus, their rebirth in heaven is immutable. That is '*unmoved karma*' (不動業).

If the things we do and the words we say are in harmony with social ethics and morality, then these are '*virtuous karma*'. Conversely, if what we do and say is socially unethical and immoral, then that is '*evil karma*'. There is yet another kind of karma which is neither virtuous nor evil. Words and deeds that follow the middle path and cause neither happiness nor suffering are called '*neutral karma*' (無記業).

In conclusion, any impurity of three karmas of body, speech and mind causes non-virtuous deeds to be committed, which result in retributive suffering for the individual and his family, or the society and our world. Thus, this human sea of suffering, an evil world stained with the five turbidities[15] is created. Death is then followed by descent into the animal realm, ghost realm and hell (going as far as to avīci, the hell of ceaseless suffering), where retributive suffering of the three evil realms must be borne. If we all have faith in Buddha, learn from and emulate the Buddha, cultivate ourselves, recite the Buddha's name, practise to eradicate our negativity and perform all that is virtuous, then with the Buddha constantly in mind, our mind karma purifies; with Buddha's name often upon our lips, our speech karma purifies; while performing actions which benefit people, our body karma purifies. With such purity of our three karmas, we should still maintain our self-awareness as we are exhausting our karmic seeds from our past. Thus, Buddha's radiance is revealed. If every one of us practises as such, our Sahā world[7] changes into utmost bliss and transforms from defiled land to a pure land.

The above is summarised by the following three charts:

THREE IMPURE KARMAS

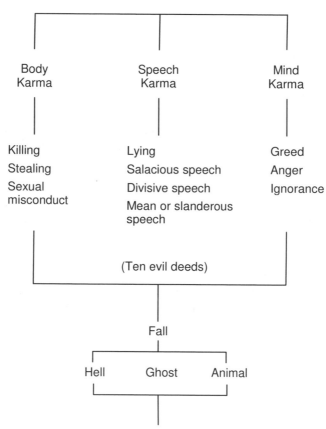

Karmic causes for descent to three evil realms

THREE PURE KARMAS

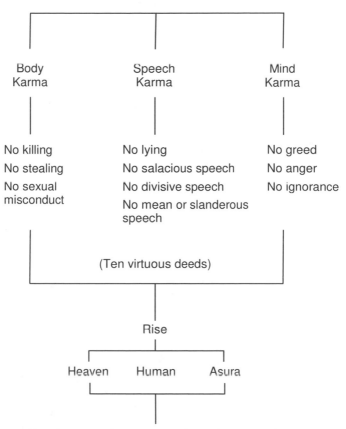

Body Karma

Speech Karma

Mind Karma

No killing
No stealing
No sexual misconduct

No lying
No salacious speech
No divisive speech
No mean or slanderous speech

No greed
No anger
No ignorance

(Ten virtuous deeds)

Rise

Heaven   Human   Asura

Karmic causes for ascent to three virtuous realms

2 KINDS OF THOUGHTS WHICH CAUSE EFFECTS

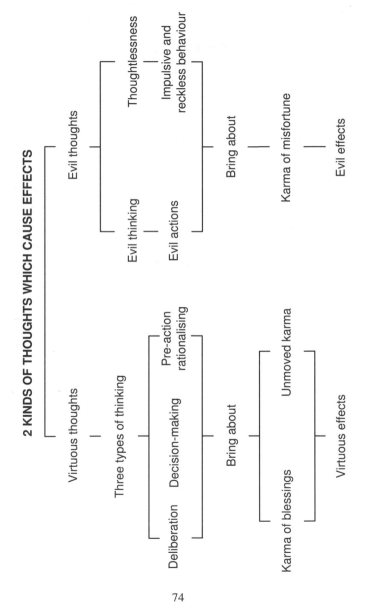

CHAPTER 10

Karmic fruit

'Cause' is the reason and *'effect'* is the result, which is also known as *'karmic fruit'*. Karma are the actions that we commit. The result produced by the karma we commit is therefore called karmic fruit.

The Law of Cause and Effect is undeniable. Experts in the field of legal studies especially value and emphasise the existence of the Law of Cause and Effect. For instance, if Charles murders somebody, they will definitely not punish Lindsey. The offence has its deserving owner, which in this case is Charles. Out of greed, anger, foolishness, desire, suspicion, etc, he planned to murder someone. That was the cause. Having purchased a dangerous weapon and killed someone is the effect. Let's explain further. Murdering a person is the cause, and receiving legal punishment will be the effect. Cause and effect spans the three periods. In the past, Charles' motive to kill was the cause. Sure enough, in the present, he murders somebody. Thus, in the future, he will definitely be punished. That will be the effect. Just as it is for a farmer; having sown seeds of melons, he reaps melons. Having sown seeds of beans, he reaps beans. Seeds sown of bitter fruit will not yield harvests of sweet fruit. Soya beans planted in the ground will never produce mung beans.

All of our daily behaviour and conduct are constantly subjected to the Law of Cause and Effect. Because of thirst and hunger, we feed. Because of fatigue, we sleep. Because of illness, we seek medical treatment. Because of livelihood, we work. Because of survival, we strive. Conscientious students have outstanding grades. They graduate to progressively higher levels of education, create for themselves brilliant futures and enjoy the fruit of blissful lives. A farmer reaps harvests because of his farming. Buildings constructed by workers who cut corners will surely collapse in the future. There is an ancient saying, *"To know of past causes, look at all that we bear in our present life. To know of future effects, examine all our actions in this present life"*. Nothing can go beyond the scope of cause and effect. However, being human, we are different from wild beasts in that we are endowed with an intuitive ability to differentiate between virtue and vice, and to abandon vice for virtue. Even a three-year old child likes beauty and dislikes evil. So as youths and adults, we should know better to distance from vices, embrace virtues, refrain from evil actions and perform virtuous deeds. Virtue or vice, both create karma, which in turn bring the consequences called karmic effects.

There is a common saying, *"Good begets good, evil begets evil. What comes around goes around. If it hasn't come back around, it's only because the time has yet to come."*

And another saying goes, *"If a do-gooder receives no good outcome, it is because he has done something bad in the past. When the misfortune has ended, good will come. Similarly, if an evil-doer does not have a bad outcome, it is because he has done something good in the past. When his blessings have been exhausted, bad will come."*

'Cause and Effect' is an undeniable Truth. Only the minority who do not believe it will dare to kill, commit arson, engage in lawless activities and break the moral principles of human relations. But eventually, they too will find that they cannot break free from the ironclad rules of cause and effect. Their present wrong-doings are creating the cause. Their future retribution of suffering will be the effect. Whoever clearly understands causes and recognises the effects will take karmic fruit very seriously. Even Jesus Christ said, *"He who lives by the sword dies by the sword"* (Matthew 26:52), which similarly demonstrates this Buddhist teaching of cause and effect. The Law of Cause and Effect is supported by Christianity as well as other religions; otherwise, why would they be encouraging virtuous deeds?

Buddhism is a religion that places great importance on the causes and effects of virtue and vice. As such, it is a very suitable practice for people of our free world. Buddhas and Bodhisattvas are very clear about cause and effect. Ancient enlightened masters said, *"Bodhisattvas are wary of cause, while sentient beings are wary of effect"*. Because the Bodhisattva has a pure mind, he is aware of the effects in advance. Being aware that a cause is evil, he does not create it. This is called being *'wary of cause'*. Most sentient beings are unclear about cause and effect. Thus they engage in lawless activities and create a lot of bad karma. Only when negative karmic fruit take effect do they begin to be worried. But by then it is already too late for regrets. This is called being *'wary of effect'*.

I hope that everyone clearly understands the principles of cause and effect, karma and its retribution; that we will all refrain from committing negative causes and thus not receive negative retributions. Let us do good deeds throughout our whole lifetime and enjoy the virtuous karmic fruit of happiness on earth and in heaven. That is bliss.

CHAPTER 11

Why do people bear consequences according to their karma?

On one occasion, 1250 Bhiksus[8], many Great Bodhisattvas, and countless lay people and celestial beings were gathered at Karanda-venurana in the City of Rājagrha, reverently listening to Buddha expounding the Dharma. At that time, Bimbisāra, the king of Magadha was also in the audience. After Buddha had completed his sermon about the sublime Dharma of Self Attainment, the king rose from his seat, reverently prostrated himself before Buddha, circumambulated the Buddha thrice, kneeled and placed his palms together. He asked the Buddha, "World-honoured One, when sentient beings commit virtuous or evil karma, the actions disappear once they have been done. Why is it that at the brink of death, whatever they have previously done appears in their minds and according to their karma, they bear the effects? The nature of all things and events is essentially empty. Sentient beings do all kinds of things acting on their thoughts. After they die, all should become empty. Why must the effects of their karma be borne? Why do karmic effects not vanish? May the World-honoured One empathise with my ignorance and explain this to me."

Buddha told the king, "Let us reflect on this example. In his dreams, a man sees a gorgeous woman and makes love to her. When he awakens, he recalls the pretty woman fondly. Your majesty, do you think what happened in the dream was real?"

The king replied, "It was not real, World-honoured One, because what appears in dreams is the result of our wishful thinking during the day. In wakefulness, they are gone. Where is that pretty woman to have fun with?"

Buddha said, "Your majesty, it is indeed as you say. The images in the dream are all illusory. They are not real. When people commit virtuous or evil actions, that is also like dream imagery, which has no nature by itself. When a man sees a beautiful lady, his sexual desire will be aroused and he will lust for her. When craving has arisen, he will find ways to get her, by hook or by crook. If he cannot fulfil his heart's desire, then love will transform to hatred, even to the extent that he will commit evil deeds which not only harm others but himself as well. Through body, speech and mind, evil deeds are committed. These evil karma are the causes for misfortunes, and they are stored in the eighth consciousness (also known as ālaya-consciousness or ālaya-vijñāna[4]) awaiting an appropriate time for fruition.

"After a deed is done, it does not vanish into emptiness without consequence or retribution. At death, when the sixth mind consciousness is on the brink of cessation, the virtuous or evil karmic seeds stored in the eighth consciousness from actions committed throughout one's lifetime, will be revealed. According to one's transgressions or blessings, one bears one's own karmic effects. It is like people startling awake from a dream. Although the illusory dreamscape is no longer visible, the stored seeds of habitual tendencies are not lost. When the seventh consciousness in this life ceases and subsequent consciousness arises, there will be cyclic transmigration in the realms of heaven, human, asura, ghost, animal and hell, i.e. within the six realms of transmigration. Your majesty, this is because there is no cessation of the virtuous or evil karmic seeds that were planted in one's previous life. This thus brings about karmic fruition in the life to come.

"In this present life, when the sixth mind consciousness ceases, it is called 'death'. When seventh consciousness arises, the next life has come. However, when the sixth mind consciousness ceases, it goes nowhere. And when seventh consciousness arises, it comes from nowhere. Why is that so? This is because the nature of consciousness is essentially empty.

"When the mind consciousness ceases, the nature of mind consciousness is empty; when the seventh consciousness (also known as manas-consciousness or manas-vijñāna[16]) ceases, the nature of seventh consciousness is empty; when the subsequent consciousness arises, the nature of the subsequent consciousness is empty; for all karma that is created, their karmic nature is essentially empty; where there is arising, the nature of arising is empty. Then, as the discriminating mind arises, thoughts stream one after another and we bear karmic effects in future lives.

"From this, we see that all sentient beings are being obscured by ignorance. We do not know the illusion of all things and events, that their nature is essentially empty. We thus greedily crave and cling, causing transmigration in cycles of birth and death."

When the Buddha reached this point, King Bimbisāra was able to understand completely. The assembly of Bhiksus, Bodhisattvas and countless lay people, celestial beings, dragons and deities listened joyfully, respectfully received the teachings and practised accordingly.

CHAPTER 12

Why do we dream?

What are dreams? Visions that are induced in our sleep are called 'dreams'. The manifestations in our dreams are not real, in the same sense that the many phenomena of our world have no real nature.

According to Samantapāsākikā (善見律), dreams fall into four categories:

1.   Dreams caused by imbalance of four elements

Our bodies are false bodies aggregated from the four elements of earth, water, fire and wind. If we dream of landslides, or soaring through space, or being pursued by tigers, wolves, robbers or thieves, these result from the four elements of earth, water, fire and wind being out of balance, so our mental state becomes dissipated. Thus, we dream these dreams.

2.   Dreams caused by previous sights

Dreams that are formed according to sceneries, things and events that we have seen during the day or night.

3.   Dreams caused by heavenly beings

If people do virtuous deeds, heavenly beings will manifest good dreams to them so that their virtuous roots will grow further. When evil people dream, heavenly beings will manifest nightmares so that they will be horrified and embrace virtuous thoughts and do good deeds.

4. *Dreams caused by thinking*

Those who are always thinking often have dreams that relate to their thoughts. If they think about virtuous matters, they have good dreams. If they think about evil matters, they have nightmares.

I would generally divide causes and formation of dreams into ten categories:

1. *Dreams caused by form*

Because in our present and past, by our faculty of sight, we have seen sceneries, things, events and colours in our world, thus dreams are formed.

2. *Dreams caused by feelings*

Because of all the feelings in our present and past, such as feelings of anguish, feelings of happiness, feelings that are neither painful nor happy, etc, dreams are therefore formed.

3. *Dreams caused by thinking*

Because we are always thinking about the past and the future, reminiscing, having wishful plans and even indulging in fantasies, dreams are therefore formed.

4.   *Dreams caused by mental activity*

Because of all that we have done through our body, speech and mind, or because our body and mind are exhausted from too much travelling during the day or overworking, dreams are therefore formed.

5.   *Dreams caused by consciousness*

Dreams that are formed by all that we have distinguished in our past and present.

6.   *Dreams caused by illness*

Because of the imbalance of the four elements (earth, water, fire and wind) of our body, various ailments occur and cause dreams.

7.   *Dreams caused by past karma*

Dreams caused by all the virtuous and evil karmic seeds that have been stored in our eighth consciousness (also known as ālaya-consciousness or ālaya-vijñāna[4]) through aeons of past rebirths.

8.   *Dreams caused by karmic effect*

Because we bear all the karmic causes that we have created in our past, this can bring about a premonition of the retributive effects that are to happen in future, which forms dreams.

9.   *Dreams caused by emotions*

Because we are bound to worldly emotions such as affection between family members, romantic love and strong friendship between people, therefore physical separation brings about a stimuli-response (感應) which forms dreams.

10. *Dreams caused by compassionate response (感應) from enlightened beings*

For the sake of purifying the world, guiding and emancipating beings; Buddhas, Bodhisattvas, sages and enlightened ones are always caring for sentient beings. Thus, dreams are manifested by the enlightened beings' compassionate response.

According to the Mahāprajñāpāramitā-śāstra (智度論), there are five types of factors that cause dreams:

1. If the body is not in harmony and you are unwell, dreaming will occur.

2. If your body has too much heat energy, you will dream of fire, yellow or red colours.

3. If your body has too much cold energy, you will dream of water or white colour.

4. If your body has too much wind energy, you will dream of yourself soaring, or of black colour.

5. If you are always thinking, you will also dream. You will either dream of past or future events.

These five kinds of dreams are illusory. They are not real events.

In the Vibhāsā-śāstra (毘婆沙論), there are also teachings which relate to dreams. Five kinds of conditions cause dreams to occur:

1. *Dreams can be induced by external factors,* e.g. by heavenly beings or ghost deities, incantations or drugs, affections and longings for family, or the guidance of enlightened beings and virtuous sages.

2. *Dreams can be induced by our past,* i.e. they can be a replay of our past encounters or actions.

3. *Dreams can be induced by what is going to happen,* i.e. if something auspicious or something terrible is about to occur, it first appears in our dreams.

4. *Dreams can be induced by our discriminating mind,* e.g. from our contemplations, hopes and cravings, misgivings and anxieties. All our various kinds of discriminations encourage more dreams.

5. *Dreams can be induced by illnesses,* i.e. if we are ill because our body's circulating life energy, blood, tendons, bones, muscles and skin have an imbalance of heat and cold, then we will have dreams.

People in this world are not the only ones who have dreams. Sentient beings of the six realms[5] also have dreams. Not only ordinary people dream; sages and enlightened beings also have dreams. Those among the enlightened ones, from stream-enterer[17] to Arahat[18], Pratyekabuddha[19] and Bodhisattva, also have dreams. Only Buddhas do not have dreams.

Why is it that after attaining Buddhahood, one has no dreams? This is because dreams are similar to delusions. As Buddha has completely eradicated all habitual tendencies of delusions, he has no dreams.

While awake, if a practitioner has no delusions about his mind and thoughts, then while he is sleeping, he will not have dreams.

During Śākyamuni Buddha's time, there was a country in ancient India named Śrāvastī. The king, Prasenajit, had ten dreams which he asked Buddha to interpret. The following are the interpretations:

1st dream

There are two bottles. One is empty and the other is full of water. Someone holds one bottle in each hand and tries to pour water from the full bottle into the empty one. But strangely, the water does not go into the empty bottle.

Explanation: This signifies that in the future, there will be wealthy people who are only willing to bequeath their wealth to their own descendents, but unwilling to give to the poor.

2nd dream

The horse's mouth and rear are stuffed with food.

Explanation: This signifies that in future, ministers will be corrupt and not only take from government officials, but also from the citizens.

3rd dream
Tree saplings bearing flowers.

Explanation: This signifies that in future, when people turn 30, they will be white-haired.

4th dream
Tree saplings bearing fruit.

Explanation: This signifies that in future, females will have babies at a very young age.

5th dream
Sheep eating rope.

Explanation: This signifies that in future generations, when the husband is out on business trips, the wife will be at home having affairs with other men, spending her husband's money and eating his food.

6th dream
Fox sitting on a golden bed.

Explanation: This signifies that in future, people of low caste will be wealthy.

7th dream
There are mature cattle that suckle milk together with calves.

Explanation: This signifies that in future, there will be a type of men who are willing to live with whores, look after home for them and live on their money from prostitution.

8th dream
Four heads of cattle charge from four directions to fight, but they disperse before even starting to fight.

Explanation: This signifies that people of future generations will advocate self-indulgence, with no fear of the justice of nature. At a time of drought, despite getting a rain master to pray for rain, they will only see clouds coming from the four directions, but it will not rain and the dark clouds will soon disperse.

9th dream
There is a large lake on a hillside with murky water in its middle and clear water at its four sides.

Explanation: This signifies that in the future, there will be chaos in the central land of earth, and peace in the surrounding eight directions.

10th dream
The flow of a large stream turns red.

Explanation: This signifies that in future, there will be emperors who send soldiers to kill and to fight. Blood will flow as a river.

In the Lotus Sūtra's Chapter of Peaceful Practices[20] (法華經的安樂行品), it is written that if a person accomplishes the four peaceful ways of practice, these five good images will appear in his dreams:

1. Vision of Buddha expounding Dharma to sentient beings.

2. Vision of oneself expounding Dharma to sentient beings.

3. Vision of Buddha confirming the future enlightenment of a practitioner.

4. Vision of people practising the Bodhisattva Way.

5. Vision of oneself fulfilling the eight aspects of a Buddha's life[21].

Stories about dreams are too numerous to mention individually. But in any case, whether dreams are beautiful or horrible, they are creations of the mind. After all, all phenomena in this world are creations of the mind, much less dreams. Dreams are illusory. If our state of mind is pure, our dreams will be virtuous. If there is evil in our mind, our dreams will be non-virtuous. We ought to encourage everyone to cultivate virtue, to refrain from all evil acts and perform many virtuous deeds. Thus, they will never have nightmares.

ಬಂ

CHAPTER 13

Everything is created by the mind

Q. What is the meaning of *'when mind arises, things and events arise; when mind ceases, things and events cease'*?

A. Everything is created by the mind. For example, if you think of doing something virtuous and act accordingly, it follows that good things will be produced. If you think, "Doing good is not beneficial, I don't want to do it anymore", then those thoughts cease and so do all the good things. Buddhist practitioners should be constantly aware of what their minds are thinking of. In a split second, many thoughts would have arisen. If all that you think of is good, then you will do good. If all that you think of is bad, then you will do bad. Everything that sentient beings do comes from the mind. Our world is extremely chaotic because of the unwholesome or evil actions that have come about from the human mind. If Buddhist practitioners want to clearly understand the mind and see their innate nature, they need to observe their mind everyday and see how the thoughts arise. Thereupon, they will know it all to be *sentient-being's mind* (the stream of arisings and ceasings of thoughts). In order to achieve a pure mind, we have to maintain the state of no arising and ceasing of thoughts.

৪৩

CHAPTER 14

We are responsible for what we are

Often we may notice that those who have faith in Buddhism but lack good understanding of it, tend to irrationally lay blame on Buddha whenever misfortune befalls them or their families. They find fault with Buddha for failing to answer their prayers and for not rewarding their faith with divine protection. They argue that it is unfair how they suffer tragedies while evil-doers are safe from disasters and lead wonderful lives. As a result, those who are influenced by such misunderstandings gradually lose their faith, deviate from their path or embrace other religions. Actually, this happens because these people have incorrect beliefs, they have yet to learn from wise teachers, their own wisdom has yet to unfold, they are still unclear about the Buddha's teachings and are losing themselves in superstition. Sigh! This is regrettable indeed.

As a matter of fact, of all the things and events that come into being in this world, there is not a single one that is not produced by an aggregation of causes and conditions. The blessings and misfortunes of any individual are also subject to the natural Law of Cause and Effect, rather than to some other power that can manipulate or alter the fate of an individual.

With regards to the Law of Cause and Effect, consider the springs and summers when the farmer tills the land, sows the seeds, clears the weeds and fertilises the crop. Because of his hard work, when autumn comes, there is a bountiful harvest to be reaped. Farming is the *cause* and the harvest, the *effect*. As Buddhist practitioners, we practise diligently so as to attain pure and unobstructed wisdom, and aspire for supreme Buddhahood while practising the Bodhisattva Way to awaken other beings. In future, when our merits[13] and virtues are complete, we will surely attain Buddhahood. In aspiring towards Buddhahood, learning from enlightened ones, cultivating ourselves, guiding others to awakening and practising the Bodhisattva Way, we plant the *cause*. Once our self-awakening, awakening of others and practice of the Bodhisattva Way have reached perfect completion, we become Buddha. This is the *effect*. These are the cause and effect of learning and practising Buddhism.

Law of Cause and Effect spans the three periods: past, present and future. The sūtras state that, *"To know of past causes, look at all that we bear in our present life. To know of future effects, examine all our actions in this present life"*. The blessings or misfortunes that we experience in our present life are a testimony to our good or bad karmic causes committed in our past lives. The karmic causes that we plant in our present life, good or bad, will produce its effects when future conditions ripen. Each virtuous or evil action does not necessarily produce its effect immediately. Hence the old adage, *"All virtue and evil will ultimately have their consequences, it is only a matter of time."*

Nobody can deny the existence of the Law of Cause and Effect. As the saying goes, *"Sow melon seeds and harvest melons; sow bean seeds and harvest beans."* One who performs deeds of virtue ascends to heaven; one who commits evil deeds descends to hell. One has to bear the consequences of one's own actions. All actions will have their effects and it is impossible for another to bear the consequences on one's behalf.

It is not only ordinary folk like us who are unable to escape the Law of Cause and Effect, karmic forces and retributions. Even enlightened beings cannot change the karmic hindrances that they themselves have created in their past lives. Karmic effects do not disappear until they have been borne. It is only by not creating new causes that we can prevent their effects.

The following is a story that illustrates how Śākyamuni Buddha had to face the retribution of his karma committed in his past life:

"Devadatta was of the Śākya clan. He was the son of King Dronodana-raja and brother of the Venerable Ānanda, who was also a younger cousin of Śākyamuni Buddha. Devadatta was a well-built and handsome man. He was a martial arts exponent, a brave and good fighter, who was also widely considered to be remarkably talented. Unfortunately, he was also conceited, arrogant, narrow-minded, petty and jealous of those who were virtuous or better than himself. When he was younger, he used to challenge Prince Siddhārtha (Śākyamuni Buddha before he became Buddha) in martial arts, but he always lost. In his heart, he was resentful and yearned to defeat the prince.

In the year that Prince Siddhārtha became Buddha, he returned to teach the royalty and ordain them as monks. Devadatta and several of his relatives followed suit and also became members of the Sangha[22] Order. However, although Devadatta had shaven his head and donned the robe of a Buddhist monk, he could not bring himself to humbly learn from Buddha's teachings. He was not diligent in his spiritual practice. Neither did he cultivate his conduct and disposition, nor attempt to emulate the Buddha in his practices. On the contrary, he was proud and self-indulgent. He wilfully hatched a conspiracy and instigated the ignorant novices to murder Buddha in order for him to take over as the 'new Buddha' and fulfil his selfish desire to usurp the position as leader of the Sangha Order.

One day, Devadatta found out that Buddha had to pass by the foot of Grdhrakuta Mountain whilst on his teaching tour. He set up an ambush and waited at the top of the hill. As Buddha passed, he pushed a huge rock down the hill, intending to crush him to death. However, Buddha is a fully enlightened one who has reached perfect completion in self-awakening, awakening of others and practice of the Bodhisattva Way. There are virtuous deities protecting him at every moment. At the crucial moment, Jin-Pi-Luo, the deity of Grdhrakuta Mountain appeared. Advancing with one extended palm, he blocked the boulder, thereby saving Buddha from a fatal incident. However, a fragment of the falling rock hit Buddha's toe and drew blood."

At this point we may be surprised. How could Buddha, unparalleled in his ubiquitous transcendental power, be subjected to such harm? Buddha had once said, "The myriad of things and events take place because of causes and conditions. The combination of these two factors brings about the fruition. This is what is known as the aggregation of causes and conditions." Thus was the cause behind Buddha's injury.

It is recorded in the Xìng-Qǐ-Sì-Xíng Sūtra (興起四行經) that in a past era, there lived a wealthy man by the name of Sutan in the city of Rajagrha. By his wife and concubine, he fathered two sons. The older of the two was named Sumati and the younger, Yaśas. The family lived happily and harmoniously. Unfortunately, one day the father became seriously ill. Realising that his time was nearing, he summoned his two sons and conveyed his last wishes to them. He emphasised that his estate was to be shared equally between the two brothers. But as soon as the father had passed away, Sumati, the elder son, had evil intentions. He planned to take advantage of his younger brother's youth and naivety, and keep the entire estate for himself. With a treacherous ruse in mind, he tricked his younger brother up an isolated mountain, onto a high precipice. Just when his brother was off guard, he pushed him off the cliff. He then climbed down the winding valley to make sure that his brother was dead. Alas, at the bottom of the cliff, he found Yaśas still breathing. Ruthless and blinded by his greed, he picked up a rock and bashed his younger brother in the head, killing him. This act was executed in extreme secrecy. Nobody ever found out about it.

The elder brother, Sumati, is Śākyamuni Buddha in this lifetime, and the younger brother is Devadatta. In this lifetime, with the meeting of these enemies, came the fruition of the retribution. From these two stories, we can see that Buddha's injury inflicted by Devadatta's rock was the result of the causality of his karma of a previous existence.

As a consequence of his evil karma through his spate of greed and killing, not only had Buddha to suffer tens of thousands of years of retributive suffering in hell in his past lives, but even as a Buddha in this lifetime, with all his full and complete merits and virtues, he was still unable to escape the Law of Cause and Effect. Even though he avoided the misfortune of being killed by the large rock, he still had to suffer the mishap of a bleeding toe. From this, we can see that cause and effect are like an object and its shadow. There are no virtuous deeds unrewarded with blessings, and no evil deeds without negative retributions. The effects of karma are not something that even enlightened beings can avoid, much less ordinary folk like us.

It is stated in the sūtras that *"Karma does not perish, not even with the passing of a hundred thousand aeons. When cause meets the right condition, one has still to bear the effect."* The retributions of cause and effect are indeed chilling. Even Buddha who had already eradicated all evil and fulfilled innumerable virtues was of no exception, let alone people like us, who are stubborn and defiant. Although we may have embraced Buddhism, we constantly continue to foolishly engage in greed, anger, ignorance, killing, stealing and sexual misconduct, thus creating heavy and deep-rooted negative karma for ourselves.

Therefore, from this day onwards, let us take responsibility for ourselves and never again blame other people, the heavens or Buddha for our misfortunes. We must diligently eradicate unwholesome actions, do good and purify the three karmas of our body, speech and mind. We must try not to plant any evil causes. This is the best way to avoid negative retributions and ensure lasting peace and harmony.

Endnotes

[1] **Five precepts**:
   1. No killing
   2. No stealing
   3. No sexual misconduct
   4. No lying
   5. No consumption of intoxicants

[2] **Ten virtuous deeds**:
   1. No killing
   2. No stealing
   3. No sexual misconduct
   4. No lying
   5. No salacious speech
   6. No divisive speech
   7. No mean or slanderous speech
   8. No greed
   9. No anger and hatred
   10. No foolishness and ignorance

[3] **Tathāgata** (如來): One who has attained full realisation of 'suchness' or true reality (Tathā-ta 眞如); i.e. become one with the absolute (Dharma-kāya), so that he 'neither comes from anywhere nor goes anywhere'; a title or epithet of Buddha.

[4] **Ālaya-vijñāna**: The eighth consciousness, being the 'storehouse' consciousness, acts as the receptacle in which

the imprints of past experience and karmic actions are stored. From it the remaining seven consciousnesses arise and produce all present and future modes of experience in *samsāra. At the moment of enlightenment, the ālaya-vijñāna is transformed into the perfect mirror-like awareness of a Buddha.

[*samsāra: *The cycle of repeated birth and death that individuals undergo in accordance with their karma until they attain nirvāna. Blinded by the three roots of evil, namely greed, anger and ignorance, sentient beings wander in samsāra until such time as they are fortunate enough to hear the Dharma, put it into practice, attain enlightenment and liberate themselves.*]

[5] **Six realms**:
1. Heaven realm
2. Asura realm
3. Human realm
4. Animal realm
5. Ghost realm
6. Hell realm

[6] **Five Skandhas**:
1. Form
2. Feeling
3. Thinking
4. Mental activity
5. Consciousness

[7] **Sahā world**: This world which is full of suffering. The Sanskrit word 'Sahā' means endurance. According to the

sūtras, the Sahā world is so called because people in this world endure much suffering stemming from the three poisons of greed, anger and ignorance, as well as earthly desires.

[8] **Bhiksu**: A Buddhist monk, an ordained member of the Sangha[22].

[9] **Kalpa**: An eon; a measurement of time widely used in ancient India.

[10] **Śramana**: A Buddhist monk.

[11] **Mara**: Symbolic of all that terminates a person's wisdom-life, hinders virtuous deeds, creates chaos for people and damages practitioners and monasteries.

[12] **Kōan** (公案): Sometimes referred to as 'Zen riddles', kōans are brief stories or dialogues from the Ch'an/Zen tradition upon which students focus during their meditation in order to penetrate their meaning.

[13] **Merit**: The state of non-arising and non-ceasing of the mind. When one attains this state, all deeds performed are with a pure, enlightened mind, free of Three Minds and Four Forms. Such deeds are meritorious.

[14] **Dhyāna-samādhi** (禪定): When all the thinking and thoughts are completely purified to emptiness, our original pure nature is revealed. This original pure nature is sustained and unmoved.

[15] **Five turbidities** of the world:
1. the defilement of the trends of the present age; 劫濁 the kalpa in decay (kalpa-kasāya), when it suffers deterioration and gives rise to the ensuing form;
2. the defilement of wrong views 見濁 (drsti-kasāya);
3. the defilement of afflictions 煩惱濁 (kleśa-kasāya);
4. the defilement of being a sentient being 眾生濁 (sattva-kasāya) in consequence human miseries increase and happiness decreases ;
5. the defilement of having a lifetime 命濁 (āyus-kasāya) human life time gradually diminishes to ten years.

[16] **Manas-vijñāna**: The seventh consciousness which is the subtle level of our consciousness - our *'I'*, *'my'*, our egoistic tendencies, attachments and emotions.

[17] **Stream-enterer**: The first of the four levels of progress 四果 toward the attainment of Arahatship[18] 阿羅漢.

[18] **Arahat**: Also known as 'worthy one'; one who has attained enlightenment of the highest level of the Hīnayāna. Arahats are no longer subject to rebirth in samsāra, i.e. in the cycle of birth and death.

[19] **Pratyekabuddha**: An enlightened practitioner who lives in a time when there is no Buddha, and has attained enlightenment in a previous existence through insight into conditioned arising.

[20] **Chapter of Peaceful Practices**: The fourteenth chapter of the Lotus Sūtra. In response to a question on the five turbidities[15] raised by Mañjuśrī Bodhisattva, the Buddha articulates the four *sukhavihāras*, or peaceful practices: those of bodily action (身安樂行), speech (口安樂行), thought (意安樂行) and of vows (誓願安樂行).

[21] **Eight aspects of Buddha's life**: The eight distinct periods of the Buddha's life, i.e.

1. 降兜率 Descent from the Tusita heaven.
2. 託胎 (托胎, 入胎) Entry into his mother's womb.
3. 降生 (出胎) Birth from his mother's side.
4. 出家 Leaving home to engage in spiritual practice.
5. 降魔 Subduing Mara; overcoming afflictions.
6. 成道 Attaining enlightenment.
7. 轉法輪 Turning the wheel of Dharma, or preaching.
8. 入滅 Entering nirvāna.

[22] **Sangha** (僧眾) : The community of Buddhist monks and nuns.

Blessings for your contribution
"The gift of Dharma excels all gifts."

In wisdom and blessings may you grow
Peace and happiness your life bestow
Afflictions overcome and soon disappear
Brightness and bliss shall prevail
Blessed you will be with bright descendants
Indeed, you will be filled with boundless benedictions.

This book would not have been possible if not for the devoted effort of the Dharma Translation Council of Humanity Vehicle Buddhism (Jen Chen Buddhism), and the contribution of many generous donors. It took months of dedicated labour to complete this task. Nonetheless, every member of the team worked joyously. They are ever grateful for the uncommon opportunity to contribute to a noble cause that provides the opportunity for our fellow human beings to benefit from Buddhadharma and be inspired to live blissful and meaningful lives. If you also wish to join in this effort of creating a brighter and happier place on earth, you may like to share the cost of publication and distribution. In this way, Buddha's teachings may spread far and wide so that more and more people can benefit from the brightness of wisdom, and be inspired to work in unison, to purify the human mind and build a blissful pure land for humanity.

To make a donation, please mail your cheque to:

Australia Buddhist Bliss Culture Mission
21 Woodthorpe Drive, Willetton
Western Australia 6155
Tel: (61) 8 9354 1245
Fax: (61) 8 9354 4475
Email: contact@buddhistbliss.org.au

Contributions via Telegraphic Transfer
can be remitted to:

Australia Buddhist Bliss Culture Mission
Account No: 1009 1438
Commonwealth Bank of Australia,
Canning Vale Branch (BSB) 06 6165,
Western Australia
Swift Code: CTBAAU2S
Bank Tel: (61) 8 9455 2099